Principles for Newsletters

Lessons learned from 37 years of newsletter publishing

CJ Chilvers

Get free updates for this book in my newsletter at cjchilvers.com.

Contents

Introduction

My first newsletter was about ninjas. It was 1987. I was 12.

Since that first ninja newsletter, I've been obsessed with the format, no matter how it was delivered.

A good newsletter forces clarity, brevity, and utility in a cluttered, information-dense world.

I transitioned to digital newsletters about small business and creativity in the 1990s — first on floppy discs I sent through the mail, then by email when that became possible.

I've created tiny newsletters for my own projects, and giant newsletters for some of the biggest corporations on the planet. Through multiple boom and bust cycles, no matter the size of the newsletter, some truths are constant.

These are the lessons I've written down for myself along the way, often after a failure. I hope you can put some of my mistakes to good use for your subscribers.

Email lasts.

You will have a medium that best speaks to you, but email is as universal as we've gotten online, so far.

Email newsletters have been pronounced dead and resurrected many times. Each time they come back stronger and more valuable.

You need a newsletter.

Y ou are a publisher now, whether you asked to be or not. In some form, your information, your content, and your story is out there somewhere.

Take ownership.

Publish.

If you aren't telling the story of your work, business, or life, someone else will. This is already happening in everything from social media posts to search results.

You may already publish, or want to publish, something for yourself or as a business — for fun or for profit. Publish a newsletter. It still returns, by far, the most for your investment.

All newsletters are personal.

F orget about the differences between personal and business newsletters.

Whether expressed or not, all email newsletters are — at their core — personal newsletters. Email is an intimate, one-to-one medium where the biggest companies on the planet compete for attention with notes from Grandma. Almost every challenge a newsletter publisher faces is based on the denial of this basic truth.

Trust is the currency of this medium. People trust people more than companies, organizations, or governments.

Trust resists automation. As trust in auto-generated, ad-inundated, broadcast newsletters erodes, real human names and faces will emerge as the most trusted "brands" in their area of interest or industry.

. . .

All newsletters are personal.

No one likes being thought of as a "brand," but there is a better word for it. Your brand is just your *reputation*.

Companies will face declining returns on their marketing because of eroding trust, and then have to hire or acquire trust at great expense.

You can start now for free.

That's the power of your newsletter. It's the hub for everything else you build. It's where you establish trust. It's where you create and maintain your reputation.

Start any kind of newsletter you want, but continue building relationships and trust in your name.

Build relationships.

That's what it's all about. All you need is one relationship to save or improve your projects, career, or life. Why not establish more?

Publishing is the most effective means humans have created to build high-quality relationships across vast amounts space and time. Don't waste the opportunity. Prioritizing revenue over relationships robs you of both.

High-quality relationships are what separate the wealthy from the successful.

Be human.

P eople recognize spam.

People recognize a sales pitch.

People also recognize honest, direct communication. This is where newsletters excel.

Be vulnerable.

Be human in voice, design, and process.

There is no competition for your personal voice.

It's easy to replicate a business model. It's really hard to replicate a personality.

Chances are, whatever your newsletter is about, there are many others sharing the same ideas and links. The only thing that separates them is voice.

Your voice is unique. Make sure it's reflected in what you publish.

Be real.

D on't dumb down a newsletter to fake being more human. People can recognize that as well.

Realize your customers are part of a generation that has grown up with email. They know what you're trying to do, so be real, not clever.

Be honest about the kind of email you're sending — in content, design, and tone.

- Is this a marketing email? OK, get me in and out. Make it clear.
- Is this a personal newsletter? Get me to something I care about and be vulnerable.
- Is this a regular letter from the CEO? Make it a real email from a real person.

Design like a human.

Be real.

. . .

Or don't design at all. That works too. The successes of text-only email newsletters have been impressive and consistent since the start of email marketing.

Readers simply want value. Your newsletter's design should help you deliver that value as quickly and clearly as possible.

Personalization is creepy.

Treat everyone online as if you're talking to them in real life. You are never automatically entitled to track a person.

"Hey [name]," is not personalization. It's transparent automation.

You wouldn't walk up to someone in public, call them by a name you hope is correct, make it obvious you scraped their personal information from a social profile, and pitch your latest product.

Nevertheless, that is what "personalization" has become and it's a trend that won't go away or shut up about how great it is.

I'm sure personalization works to sell more in the short term when used with a light touch. But I've never subscribed to anything because I hoped I could be sold to more.

· · ·

Personalization is creepy.

A seller-focused strategy will always lose head-to-head against a reader-focused strategy in the long run. It's a competitive opportunity too few are willing to explore.

Stop personalizing. Start humanizing.

The best metric is replies.

T he best metric in email newsletters is how many replies you receive.

The reply is the greatest advantage an upstart newsletter has.

Large organizations often discourage replies with layers of bureaucracy. They publish newsletters to nameless, faceless audiences, that need to remain that way, or their process breaks down.

You have the advantage of building relationships with your audience one-on-one and pivoting immediately based on real-time feedback. Use it.

No one cares.

You have to give them reasons to care.

Earn five seconds of their attention.

Then, earn the next five.

Repeat.

Just start.

You can't establish relationships if you're not out there. Whatever it takes, get your idea out there now. Course correct, if and when needed.

It's impossible to learn from or improve a newsletter until it exists. So, just start.

No one is going to care for long while, so feel free to make mistakes. Every failure is potential content for the future.

Perfection sucks and it's boring.

Curate.

There are way too many creators and not enough editors. The current crush of mediocre content will only increase. We need picky people with fine-tuned bullshit detectors to comb through it all and surface the good stuff.

The curation newsletter format, linking to the best of the best with a little personal commentary, works because your readers are looking for answers for multiple microproblems within a topic. It's never just one.

Think of it as a lottery. You can try to get attention from a headline and have one chance to connect with your readers. Or you can offer several interesting headlines, from multiple sources including yourself, increasing your odds that something will speak to your reader enough to be considered useful.

Sharing useful information is powerful. Finding the best content fills your personal network with the best creators. It does the same for readers. There's nothing more valuable than being the hub of all those connections.

Curate.

. . .

Curate your archives as strategically as your newsletter. Your archives are the searchable, text-based representation of the network hub you've built. Readers don't search chronological archives on websites like they did decades ago. Repurpose that archive to create guides, books, podcasts, and videos — whatever forms of media your audience prefers to consume.

Your archive is the foundation for your future products and services. Keep it useful. Keep it curated.

But understand that curation is hard.

A useful, curation-based newsletter is more difficult to publish than any other kind of newsletter.

- It takes longer.
- It requires a defined process over time to be consistent.
- It requires deep knowledge of the subject matter.
- It requires the interest, time, and effort to seek out the highest-quality links.
- It requires enough knowledge of a community to know which links are the most valuable to the reader.

Curation favors individual humans being useful to other individual humans. It's the simplest form of content in concept. It's the hardest to execute in practice. It's an enormous opportunity for creators who want to stand out.

Be consistent.

W hy do mediocre creators often get more attention than the best creators?

The hardest problem to solve in creating anything for the public is consistency.

Take podcasts as an example. Depending on your source, there's an estimated 5 million podcasts in existence. But only about 500,000 are active (published the last 90 days), with much fewer being consistently active (on a regular schedule).

The same was true of blogging in its heyday. The same is true of video and email newsletter publishers today.

Consistency is an orders-of-magnitude-level differentiator.

. . .

Be consistent.

Attention comes and goes in seconds. Consistency is how you maintain attention.

Humans are creatures of habit. Become a part of their routine.

Everything is an essay.

For most new newsletters, I don't suggest starting with a curation-based newsletter. I suggest starting with the "essay" format first.

It's all about what you're trying to solve for in the moment. Most newsletters need to solve for consistency in the beginning. This is when the humble essay can be your best friend.

Anything can be an essay. It's the most versatile format of publishing. Link posts, quotes, photos, videos, a Q&A, or just paragraphs of ideas — it can all be formatted as an essay. Essays can be a sentence or book in length. Whatever length keeps you creating and your subscribers reading is the perfect length.

Essays are less work than curation. You should aim to eventually do both, by publishing essays and linking to them as you would anything else in your curated newsletter. But curation takes more time and experience. Worry about consistency first.

. . .

Everything is an essay.

Essays are important to have in your archive when creating products, podcasts, videos, books, and courses years down the road. They're far easier to compile into collections, like the one you're reading now.

Essays also give you a bit more room to be creative and human. No matter how you choose to humanize your content (adding audio, video, social posts, or streams), it's easy to embed it in an essay.

Best of all, the essays you create will become the links used in other publishers' curation newsletters. They'll happily send readers your way. Everybody wins.

Be brave. Be brief.

B revity is considerate, difficult, and valuable.

Concise writing takes more work, but it's more likely to be read.

Most books should be a blog post. Most blog posts should be a social post. Most social posts shouldn't be.

Conquer email obesity. Deliver maximum value per pixel.

Deliver value.

Solve someone else's problem — the bigger the better.

It's nice if it solves your problem too.

Create daily.

Y ou don't have to publish daily, but creating daily is the process that makes everything else possible. You can also call it a "practice," because it takes lot of repetition to refine and it's never perfect.

How you refine your creative practice will be as individual as our brains, no matter how many one-size-fits-all systems are being sold to you.

I can't tell you what your creative practice should be. But I can give you the secret to quickly determining what process will work best for your brain...

When stuck, apply another constraint.

C onstraints boost creativity.

Can't write an essay? Write a paragraph. Can't write a paragraph? Write a sentence. Eventually, you will find a constraint that makes daily creation possible.

The trick for consistent newsletter publishing is finding *useful* constraints for both you and your subscribers.

What is useful to your audience?

- Getting to the point
- Finding obscure ideas, people, and resources for solving specific challenges
- Finding entertaining ideas, people, and resources
- Providing more value than you ask for in return
- Having a consistent publishing schedule

When stuck, apply another constraint.

. . .

What is not useful to your audience?

- Over-designing
- Over-formatting

What is useful for you?

- Limiting words and topics
- Limiting when or how your work is published
- Using *process*-based templates and automation
- Being imperfect
- Having a consistent publishing schedule

What is not useful for you?

- Using templates and automation that detract from your publishing voice
- Publishing and marketing based on trends
- Being acceptable to everyone

Your products are just a byproduct.

Focus on improving your daily creative practice and everything else works itself out.

The process of creating something small every day is its own reward. It keeps you consistent and sharp, while protecting against burn out.

Your newsletter, and any product derived from your newsletter, is just the byproduct of that creative practice.

There's a difference between cranking out content products as a goal and showing up every day to create something fitting your unique constraints. Both will get you to a similar place over time, but only one will keep you sane.

Be OK.

Burnout is real. It may be the #1 killer of great newsletters.

At younger ages, burnout may be a mix of overpromising, lack of self-awareness, and the lack of a willingness to experiment — perhaps brought on by social pressures.

We all need to be a lot more OK with being generalists, having hobbies, and creating our own labs online. Mostly, we all need to be more OK with being OK.

Based on the research of psychologist Raymond Cattell in the 1960s, and Harvard professor Arthur C. Brooks in the 2020s, our brains seem to transition from rewarding "fluid intelligence" (solving problems through novel innovations) to "crystalized intelligence" (solving problems through experiential wisdom) at a predictable age range (late 30s to early 40s).

. . .

Be OK.

I believe it's the failure to adapt to this change that creates a perfect environment for burnout.

Younger publishers need a lab online to try new ideas, fail, and try again. Be OK with being unsafe. Piss off people who need to be pissed off. Delight those you respect. If too many people agree with what you're saying, you're not saying anything new.

Older publishers like myself should transition to sharing the great innovations of others, adding context based on experience, and passing along what we've learned. An experienced newsletter publisher can save a business millions in the first few minutes of a consultation. An experienced business owner is well aware of this value. There's always opportunities awaiting creators who are OK with how their brain changes over time.

When I see creators "taking a break" from creating online, it doesn't look to me like they feel they have the agency or energy to pivot to something their brains are better suited for, so they just stop creating anything.

This is another good reason to have a personal newsletter — one apart from your business. You need a place to work out how your brain works. A storefront for your goods will suffer without a proper workshop in the back.

Don't automate relationships.

ll parts of the newsletter process can be automated, not all should be.

There's an uncanny valley that too many newsletters enter with complex automation schemes. The more complex the scheme, the more you begin to rely on apps to tell you who your readers are, and what your content should be.

It's best to keep your process simple for as long as possible.

Properly placed automations should occur to you over time and should never come at the cost to the relationship you have with your readers or the quality of the content.

Don't be an asshole.

Make it easy to unsubscribe.

Don't get bogged down in tracking. People are not "clicks."

Respond.

Only one person is opening this email.

You are not a broadcaster. Crowds are not gathering around a single screen to read your email.

Write to one reader.

Give a shit.

It's shocking how many don't.

Discovery is recovery.

L ooking for your next revelatory essay idea or content strategy?

You've thought about, and created around, seemingly unrelated topics a thousand times without realizing how they intersect.

Re-read what you've already created. You'll find something new every time.

No size fits all.

No matter what you do, you won't please your entire audience.

That's a good thing.

Build trust by being honest and you're bound to get hate.

Recognize what delights you about other newsletters.

I t's not necessarily what engages you. That's too easy. Machines can do that.

Engagement is good for a few sentences. Delight builds anticipation for the next issue.

You're probably not producing enough delight.

The title doesn't matter.

D on't spend a lot of time on the title (or branding) of your newsletter. Use that time for more important things, like publishing.

As time passes, if the title stops working for you, it's easy to change.

The experience makes the title.

Focus on your From line.

Subject lines don't matter anywhere near as much as your From line.

Small changes to a subject line can produce small improvements. Small changes to a From line can make or break a newsletter entirely.

The From line is the first thing a reader reads. It's big and bold above the subject line. The reader often decides the value of the email at the From line before they get to the subject line — if they get to the subject line.

Trust is the only thing that improves your From line.

Be proud of your link.

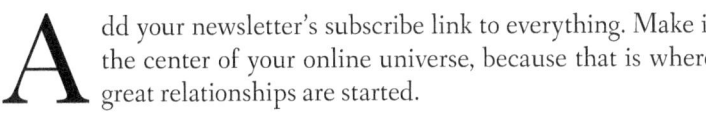

Add your newsletter's subscribe link to everything. Make it the center of your online universe, because that is where great relationships are started.

If you build a newsletter of value, it's your duty to expose it to as many readers as possible.

Put your best link forward.

W hat gets linked to first gets clicked on the most. Make this first link valuable enough for the reader to want to return to your newsletter.

It seems obvious. But it's not what I see in most newsletters. Most seem too concerned with looking good or being neatly organized by subject or type of content.

Concentrate on presenting the best of the best up front and each issue of your newsletter will be considered valuable from the start.

Cut ruthlessly.

G et to the point.

Don't be afraid to vigorously cut lower-quality content to create a higher-quality experience.

Do the same for subscribers. Don't attract "easy" subscribes from giveaways, partnerships, or whatever the latest growth trends say. Those relationships are fickle. They will cost you.

Apply this principle to your creative practice as well. Delete first. Then, edit, organize, or automate what remains.

Avoid announcements.

Your brain doesn't know the difference between announcing something and shipping it.

Announcements are easy, tempting content in newsletters. They feel good and fill up lots of space, but they don't do much for your audience or your creative output.

Announcements are also rarely compelling to readers.

If you post a product announcement or an intention to add something to your newsletter, include something compelling for the audience and something to make you accountable to your audience to actually ship what you're announcing.

Want engagement? Be engaging.

Introductions matter, whether it's in an email or in person. Your first email to a reader should invite a conversation. This helps you establish to both the email providers and to your reader that you're a real person, who cares. Plus, it's just a nice thing to do.

Make it easy to unsubscribe up front and they will feel good about coming back whenever they feel like it.

Get to know as many readers as possible one-on-one. When you meet readers in person, you get a better understanding of how what you do fits in their world. It shapes the way you publish, as well as what you publish.

If you're thinking, "This can't scale," you're dreaming of a problem that's wonderful to have, and few obtain. I've ghost-written emails for executives with audiences in the millions. They love getting feedback from individual customers and they spend hours making sure the customer is happy, while capturing their thoughts.

. . .

Want engagement? Be engaging.

Your audience should never be too enormous to talk to as real people.

Monetization is a byproduct.

I f you build an audience to serve that audience, monetization will present itself. You don't need to chase it. You don't even need to accept it if you don't want the added responsibility.

Pick a day, any day.

Every year, reports are published on the best days and times to send your newsletter. None of it represents the habits of your readers.

Your audience is not like anyone else's.

You have more control over your publishing schedule than anyone dares to admit.

Publish in a manner and at a time that best fits your habits or strategy first. Your audience will adapt, as long as you are consistent and valuable.

Ask for testimonials.

Present your potential readers with quotes praising your newsletter from names they are likely to know and trust.

How do you get these persuasive nuggets of gold? Ask.

Ask for opinions, reviews, and suggestions from all readers. You never know who'll respond. Keep an eye out on social media too. When someone says something nice about you, ask them if you can use it as a quote.

No, asking doesn't make you seem like a self-promoting blowhard. It makes you seem like someone who really values the opinion of the person being asked and the subscribers you serve.

Social proof is overrated.

"Social proof" gets too much attention. Testimonials, subscriber numbers, and boastful accomplishments have their place when marketing your newsletter, but they're often used as a crutch for bad content strategy, distracting potential subscribers.

Adding social proof is adding reassurance for a person who has already made at least one decision in your favor. They've arrived at a page or opened an email. They've read a headline and chosen to read more. They've clicked a button.

These are all incredibly important decisions and actions. They happen within seconds.

Social proof is what comes after those critical first decisions. You don't need to reassure someone about a decision before they've made a decision.

. . .

Social proof is overrated.

Why is social proof such a popular topic for the advice-givers, versus getting past that critical first few seconds?

To the publisher, social proof isn't just reassurance copy. It's a psychologically satisfying way to battle imposter syndrome, convince a boss that you're doing a good job, or convince your employees that they're helping to solve important problems.

It feels really good.

But to the reader, social proof is primarily a way of reassuring themselves about their initial decision. Social proof is important, but it's nowhere near as important as making that initial connection. Be selective in your usage.

Give more away for free.

Nothing is more valuable than the relationships you're building. Projects come and go, succeed and fail. The audience should remain. What attracts and keeps them is what you're giving away.

You're probably not giving enough away.

Inspiration is scheduled.

I t's also called work.

The common denominator of all work isn't projects, attention, or energy. It's time.

Humans are horrible at estimating time. Schedules tame your illusions about time.

Your schedule is there to keep you consistent and sane — while creating the proper amount of space to work. Your schedule is the foundation of your process.

This means scheduling time for leisure too. All work and no play makes for a boring newsletter.

. . .

Inspiration is scheduled.

Email publishers don't want to admit they're in the entertainment business, but they are. What makes you entertaining? What is entertaining to your audience?

How can you make this all a little more fun and interesting for everyone?

The workspace of the future is a workbench.

To get the most from the time you schedule for creative work, the experts — and my years of experimenting — seem to agree:

- Work in short bursts.[1]
- Work in silence.[2]
- Work in a place that is neither your personal living space, nor "the office."[3]

After decades of research and a mountain of books on the subject, we've rediscovered the concept of a workbench.

Once again, discovery is recovery.

The workspace of the future is a workbench.

Sources:

1. Inc., "For 95 Percent of Human History, People Worked 15 Hours a Week. Could We Do It Again?" September 2020.
2. The Atlantic, "The Best Music for Productivity? Silence," December 2016.
3. The New Yorker, "What if Remote Work Didn't Mean Working from Home?" May 2021.

Celebrate and share the wins of others.

B e the cheerleader for your topic.

Your competition isn't other creators. Your competition is:

- Short attention spans
- Unlimited life distractions
- Limited awareness that you exist

A win for creators in your community is a win for your community. Promote those wins. Build relationships within the community.

My longest-term readers and customers are fellow creators. That wouldn't be true if I had treated of them like competitors.

Own the experience.

O wn a piece of the internet under your own name and on your own terms. Know what your audience likes, and provide it in a way no other service can.

Beware of the value of the reputation you're lending to social media companies. Their brand is likely less trustworthy than yours. Their reputation, their brands, will come and go — but yours is for a lifetime. Treat it well.

Your site, blog, and newsletter should be 100% you. It's where you build your reputation. You own the reader experience.

It's easy these days to be everywhere. Automations exist to make distribution possible wherever your audience is, with as little or as much personal involvement and customization as you like. This creates a convenient experience, but not a great experience.

Create the best experience for your audience in a place you own. Own as much of the experience as possible.

Avoid ads.

void advertising as a business model for as long as possible.

It seems like the easiest, fastest way to monetize, especially to a younger generation who grew up idolizing YouTubers and influencers — who live and breathe the ad model.

Advertising has always been an unstable business. It's not the foundation you want to build upon. Depending on your business, it may not even be the supplemental income you want to bring in during the good times.

You own every pixel of your subscribers' experience. If you choose to cede those pixels, you are vouching for those advertisers. You may not believe you are doing that, but it's not up to you. It's up to your audience.

. . .

Avoid ads.

It's your responsibility. It's your reputation. It may not always mean legal liability, but it certainly means reputational liability.

Companies can rebrand and resurrect in a relatively short amount of time. Individuals can't.

It's a gamble.

You know what's less of a gamble?

Make your own product or service. Control the experience. Communicate directly and honestly with your audience. Repeat.

Social media is not about you.

Not every social media strategy needs to be creepy.

Send invitations to visit the nicer experience that you've built. Tag everyone you mention or link to in the newsletter.

This simple strategy has brought in more high-quality, genuinely interested readers than anything else I've ever done on social media. Everyone likes to see their name promoted by someone else. Plus, it's a great excuse for them to mention your newsletter to their followers.

The byproduct of doing thoughtful things is that sometimes thoughtful things happen back to you. This is so much better than traditional creepy social media strategies, because it's about being actually social.

.   .   .

Social media is not about you.

Sometimes this leads to someone discovering a newsletter for the first time. Sometimes it leads to discussions with additional links and ideas that are useful for future newsletters.

Everyone wins.

Don't force growth.

G rowth tactics are tempting. Every month, there seems to be a new way to game some system and enjoy a flood of new subscribers.

Resist these growth tactics, as they tend to add lots of tourists to your subscriber lists, increasing your hosting fees, and harming your deliverability potential.

There are some subscribers you don't want.

Ten thousand loyal readers will yield far better results for you than 100,000 skimmers, and for far less money.

As in most things in life, focus on quality over quantity.

False scarcity isn't scarcity.

L iterally — but it also lacks the long-term effectiveness of scarcity.

Limited-availability offers for digital products work to attract new subscribers and customers in the short term, but never as well as offering actual, real-world scarce items, like events, coaching sessions, and physical products.

Plus, it comes off as dishonest. Your newest, most active subscribers never knew a time before the internet. They know that nothing digital has limited availability, unless it's artificially imposed. It feels fake.

Consider how that reflects on your reputation.

Unlearn.

E verything changes. It's the only constant.

Be ready to unlearn when presented with new information.

About the Author

Hi, I'm C.J. I publish books and essays on creativity, publishing, and marketing. I also provide content strategy for (mostly) big-tech companies.

For 20+ years, I've published an email newsletter about the useful ideas I stumble across in my work at **cjchilvers.com**. Subscribe for updates to this book as they happen.

Thanks for reading!